War
& Love
SANA UQBA

War
& Love
SANA UQBA

SANA UQBA

ISBN: 1999586603
ISBN-13: 978-1999586607
(Sana Uqba)

AUTHOR'S NOTE

On September 21, 2014, Houthi rebels from Yemen's north-
ern city of Saada marched into the capital after forming an
alliance with the former Yemeni President Ali Abdullah Saleh.
The rebels, armed and supported by Saleh's loyalist forces,
seized control of government buildings and institutions in a
move that forced the internationally recognised government
of Abedrabbo Mansour Hadi to flee.

The following March, unwilling either to watch its neigh-
bour fall into chaos or risk its own security, Saudi Arabia
- which claims the Houthis are a proxy force of Iran, intent
on advancing Tehran's allegedly expansionist agenda - blew
the dust off its arsenal of military equipment, called up its
friends in the region, and went to war against the rebels.
Airstrikes rained down upon the capital and other parts of
rebel-held Yemen, and millions of civilians were sudden-
ly caught in a deadly battle between the Houthis and the
neighbouring Saudi kingdom, which said it aimed to restore
Hadi's legitimacy but has seemingly found itself in a contro-
versial and unwinnable scenario.

Yemen's conflict has plunged the region's poorest nation
into depths of unseen darkness. While the death toll so far
stands at more than 10,000, a further three million have
been flung to all corners of the nation and beyond, and more
than half of the country's 28.9 million people are barely
surviving.

North of Yemen is Saudi Arabia, the nation prolonging the
war. To the east is Oman, a country deemed to be a regional
mediator between warring factions. To the west is the Red
Sea, which eventually strokes the shores of Egypt– all of
which are dead-end options for civilians attempting to flee
the war-stricken country.

But like Pandora's Box, the conflict has unleashed even more fiendish characters to blight Yemen's formerly peaceful and care-free civilians. Hunger, poverty, kidnapping, airstrikes, drone strikes, sectarianism, civil war, recruitment of child soldiers, regional meddling, a collapsing economy, cholera, famine and government corruption are among the many crises to hit the country once described as 'Arabia Felix' - Happy Arabia.

Today, Yemen is a fractured nation battered by the brutal Saudi-led coalition of militaries where rebels continue to wage carnage in the capital while al-Qaeda and Islamic State group militants carve space out of the chaos to thrive in the south once more - continuously and constantly regaining the confidence to target a badly weakened security force and a failing state.

All attempts to reach a peaceful political settlement, including those backed by global powers, have failed Yemen's people time and time again. Many have simply lost hope amid the ongoing suffering.

"The situation in Yemen - today, right now, to the population of the country - looks like the apocalypse"
- Mark Lowcock, Head of the UN Office for the Coordination of Humanitarian Affairs (OCHA).

"This war is causing enormous human suffering to some of the poorest and most vulnerable people in the world, and there are no humanitarian solutions to humanitarian crises. Yemen is the world's worst humanitarian crisis."
- United Nations Secretary-General António Guterres (UN).

DEDICATION

This book is dedicated to all those who have lived through the treacherous realities of war; for those who have lost their lives, livelihoods, souls, limbs, happiness, family and peace of mind as a result.

This book is dedicated to all those on the ground who have clung on to hope and remained steadfast in their faith despite the continued struggle; for those who have attempted to heal the nation while they themselves are hurting.

This book is dedicated to the hidden members of our society that maintain integrity through the dirt; the politicians, activists and community leaders that insist on resisting, protesting and believing in the power of the people.

This book is dedicated to the local journalists that risk their lives to ensure our people remain in the headlines, and to all international journalists, especially freelancers, who work tirelessly to push the forgotten conflict to the forefront of global news.

This book is dedicated to all those in the diaspora who have held onto their roots and refused to allow the war to continue without challenging its legality, despite the pangs of hurt felt from years of absence.

This book is dedicated to our people and their allies who lay awake all night patiently praying for the coming dawn.

"Good morning," the television chants,
But our **mournings**
Are anything but
Good here.

- Sana Uqba

Where do we run
When airstrikes pound the north
Rebels reign the west
Militants threaten the south
And famine grips the east

- Sana Uqba

He wore his robe like a king
And wrapped his head with a throne,
He buckled his weapon around his waist
And placed a sweet **kiss on her crown**

- Sana Uqba

Trauma;
Absolute **trauma** all round.
Poets drop their pens
Words no longer make sense
Only tears are shed
Only screams are said
And artists?
Artists are colour blind to all
But the colour red
Musicians only play strings
On their blood-soaked violins,
Singers hardly sing
But recite lines of folklore
In sync
And what of those who sin?
They spend their nights
In prostration to The King

- Sana Uqba

The sun rose and pushed them one by one
Onto the ageing bus
Fresh bread, a little butter
And some cheese
That's all it took -
Oh and some tea
A whole lot of singing
And laughter; that's a **perfect day**
At the beach

- Sana Uqba

Jets pierced through
Her beautiful skies
Like the rapist
That injected his
Unwanted seed
Into her

- Sana Uqba

Smoke rises from the clay pot,
Incense,
The incense
Smells like royalty,
Tea is poured into a glass cup
And in the distance
The call of prayer
Seeps through the curtains
Like fresh breeze
On a spring day,
It's almost as poetic as
The dragon blood trees,
Sitting on the hilltops of Socotra.
Praise be to The Poet
Praise be to The Poet
Praise be to The Poet
- Sana Uqba

They launch every strike
With **blessings of your name**
And with every force that rocks
Our homes, Ya Allah,
We cry Your name too

- Sana Uqba

This is injustice
At its peak,
And justice is all we seek,
The whole world is watching
But **no one really sees**

- Sana Uqba

Colours of all shades on material
You've yet to imagine
The women,
The women,
They sparkle like diamonds
The smell of oud sweetens the air
The bass sends vibrations down
Your spine
Laughter and ululation intertwined
Like magic
Then it turned tragic.
Dazed,
The bass flatlined
And the only beat came from my chest,
Blood drenched the air
Nothing moved
No one breathed
Until a dusty hand rebelled against the rubble
Like weed through concrete.
She held her hand to her upper lip
Like the lipstick she decorated
Herself with
Just hours earlier,
She struggled,
But she ululated,
She ululated
"This.. is.. a.. wedding
Ya awlad al kalb," she heaved

- Sana Uqba

*Sons of bitches

10

When will they be satisfied?
"When our spirits break," he replied,
As he lit up **another cigarette**

- Sana Uqba

It's true what they say
About salt water.
I am still thirsty
For more of you,
I still crave
The flow of your ocean
Through my fingers;
The texture of your sand
Between my toes.
This land
Does not quench
My **thirst.**

- Sana Uqba

Like the cracked hands of my father,
It stands tall, proud,
Unshaken.
- Sana Uqba

Bloodshot seeping through
My cornea,
It sits on dark circles,
Even my body is turning
Red, white, black

- Sana Uqba

There he was
Must I leave him to lay?
Whisking **lonesome in the winds**
of yesterday,
As I walk into the seconds
of tomorrow

- Sana Uqba

Let us travel
To the peak of the **mountain top**
And there,
We will tell God
Everything.
Everything.

- Sana Uqba

She lay her tired hand
On her bump
While watching smoke rise above the horizon
Wondering whether
Life or death
Would be of benefit
to **her seed**

- Sana Uqba

Like headless chickens,
They climb the mountain of rubble
In search for heads and limbs,
Screaming like **detectors,**
Getting closer
And closer.

- Sana Uqba

Let leaves fall
And mountains break
And oceans gush
And missiles strike
Let death call
And quakes shake
And time rush
And ink dry.
Let the whole world
Crumble
Around
Us

- Sana Uqba

Before you question why,
Know there is wisdom in everything.
"Ma, what wisdom can you see here?"
Son, the **Prophet never lies**

- Sana Uqba

With every tick of the clock
Our lifetimes separate,
O' tears of sorrow
To him rise, evaporate,
Speak to him of **broken souls,**
Take me to him,
Levitate

- Sana Uqba

Tears steal my words
Like **rebels in the moonlight**

- Sana Uqba

Habibti, when glass breaks
You pick up those pieces
And create a **mosaic**

- Sana Uqba

I'll tell you what it's like;
Dust travels like hurricanes,
And screams distort the sirens,
But time still pauses.
See, in the **eye of the storm,**
There is no storm.

- Sana Uqba

"In our part of the world
Children who face monstrous struggles
Day in, day out
My brother, they don't fear
The **monster under the bed,"** he laughed

- Sana Uqba

Will they win?
"Do you know where you are?
Wake up and smell the **coffee.**"

- Sana Uqba

Blood seeps through
The pen of a scholar in Tarim
"So **lose not heart** nor despair," he writes
Over and over again,
Before a gentle breeze dries the ink
And a teardrop falls
From his ageing beard.
"Verily with hardship comes ease."

- Sana Uqba

The thought of peace
Brews on my mind every day
Like the coffee beans of Mokha
In my morning cup
I sip **my qahwa,**
From the rooftops of the Old City
Breathing in a sight that has blessed men
For more than two thousand years
Before me.
Peace will surely come.

- Sana Uqba

Mama, the **bad guys** always
Die in films
"Yes, son."
So why was Baba killed?

- Sana Uqba

Searching through a gaping hole
I find **smiles, laughs and broken souls**,
But with their pens and colourful markers
All they draw are bullets, guns and bombs

- Sana Uqba

I stumble down
The **hazy aisles** of the hospital.
Doctors treat impatient patients
Thrown along the corridor.
Rooms have no doors,
And no curtains separate the dead.
"Welcome to the graveyard," they said.

- Sana Uqba

Our warriors
March into the battlefield
Singing to the **tunes of doves**
And you question
Whether we want war or love?

- Sana Uqba

She grasped her backpack
As she walked down the street
"Where are you going?" her friend
Shouted from the window.
"Aren't you coming to school?" Hiba replied
"Girl, give it a rest. **We're at war.**"
"What can I say, Baba insists.
How oppressive, right?" she said,
Rolling her eyes.
"The oppression is real," her friend laughed.

- Sana Uqba

And when the machines above
Get too loud
We take a walk down the coast
For moments, crushing waves
Take us back to **normalcy**

- Sana Uqba

Under the night sky they stood
In their own **silence,**
Talking the language of love
During a time of war

- Sana Uqba

When the **lights go out,**
The monitors don't beep
And the defibrillators don't resurrect
The dead.

- Sana Uqba

"They have money"
We have heart
"They have weapons"
We have heart
"They have soldiers"
We have heart
"They ha-"
We have
Heart.

- Sana Uqba

O' rainfall don't add to these
Salty tears,
For I am drowning and thirsty

- Sana Uqba

There is **greatness**
Buried in the sands
And stories etched in the hands
Of the elders,
Every mountain top
Has witnessed
The ageing of the land,
And the sounds of each wave
Has whispered poems of love
Into the broken hearted

- Sana Uqba

What is love?
"Home"
What is home?
"You"
- Sana Uqba

I've been stripped of my hope
Stripped from my land
Tell me, what more is left for me?

- Sana Uqba

They spoke of
Humanity
And sold us
Dreams
Of a better life.
Only to **close their borders**
And block our entry
And reject our
Asylum
And shatter our
Hopes.

- Sana Uqba

Try to..
Try to open..
Try to open your eyes,
Buthaina.
Tell the world
What you saw

- Sana Uqba

The mother of a slain
Child has no time
To **debate politics**

- Sana Uqba

Don't your men carry knives?
"Don't **your bombs** kill our children?"

- Sana Uqba

Yesterday
They told us
They would wage war on us
To protect us.
Today, they shut us off
From the rest of the world
In our traditions, a **man's word**
Never changes.

- Sana Uqba

We are starving prisoners
Of conscience.
Are they aware?
Do they care?
Are they conscious?
Where is their **conscience?**

- Sana Uqba

"The kids?" he smiled.
"They count the seconds
Between the strikes
Then pounce like excited cubs
Selling **flowers to passers-by**.
Just like always."

- Sana Uqba

They say silence is deafening
And we hear **constant screams**

- Sana Uqba

On my mind a **bloody scene.**
My heart beats,
I beat my heart;
A wounded soul
I'm drowning in sorrow

- Sana Uqba

They looked me in the eye
As they made my mother bleed,
The echoes of her cries
And the echoes of her screams,
Resurrected the tides and the waves
Of the **Dead Sea**

- Sana Uqba

"Alo? How are you?"
The skies erupt,
I feel the house shake
Like an earthquake.
Screams
Cries
Chaos
I hear her raise her finger,
Wipe her tear
And sniff into the telephone.
"Alhamdulilah,"
She responds

- Sana Uqba

For a second,
Just a split second,
The rumbles above
Struck fear in my heart
But this heart
Belongs to
Balqees,
Don't you know?

- Sana Uqba

Imagine waking every morning
Knowing your name
Could be wiped
And replaced with
Just a number
In a mounting death toll

- Sana Uqba

Mother, may your soul
Rest In Peace
As my heart
Lives in **pieces**

- Sana Uqba

His white robe was bloodied with a
Hand print
In the same place
I would rest my
Hand before kissing him
Every morning

- Sana Uqba

O' world,
Echo our anthem
To all corners of the Earth,
Rock their world
With the sound of our woes
And tell them,
We are humans too

- Sana Uqba

Habibti, light up your best *bukhoor
Congratulations, you are now the proud
Mother of a martyr

- Sana Uqba

*Incense

Trees still grow
Flowers still blossom
The sea maintains its same schedule.
War cannot stop us
From living, son

- Sana Uqba

Nothing is worse
Than seeing water drown the eyes of
A defeated mother;
A woman who cannot
Speak, express, scream
That, is the sign of
True oppression

- Sana Uqba

He stumbled in like a child
Moments before worry turned into tears.
"Habibti, sorry I'm late.
I was haggling over this rose
For you."
I must be Laila,
Qais is definitely crazy

- Sana Uqba

Mama told me I'm a warrior,
She shows me her poker face
But I know she's a worrier,
I put my bag on and walked
Saw her in the corner
Of my cornea,
I'm excited for first day of school
This must be euphoria.
Ahmed waved from the bus
I boarded and left the area,
Smiles and clear skies above
We were merrier than merrier
When my teachers scolding
Was disrupted
With a silent ringing that was scarier.
Hysteria.
Terror infected our lives like bacteria,
Mama was no longer worried
Mama was delirious,
"My baby was a **warrior**
Killed by barbarians,
Justice belongs to Him
All other powers are precarious,"
She screamed among young coffins,
As shovels began
To bury us

- Sana Uqba

Welcome to the land
Where nightmares
Merge with reality
Like **salt and water.**
We wake up thirsty
Every morning

- Sana Uqba

Know that
I am far greater
Than the number
You see in **your headlines**

- Sana Uqba

Comfort sounds like a little bit
Of oud strings
And the croaky voice
of Faisal Alawi

- Sana Uqba

A gun battle exploded outside our window
He held my hand almost instantly.
And it was in that moment,
That the film we were watching
Became a little less **romantic**

- Sana Uqba

Aren't you at war?
"No, we are **always in love.**"

- Sana Uqba

I will fly,
I will rise,
Far beyond
The seven skies
Watch me
Break free
Seeking justice
I will stand,
Watch me climb
If I just spread my broken wings
I will elevate
And rise

- Sana Uqba

Poor health
Poor wealth
And here are my rich brothers
Poking at my wounds

- Sana Uqba

Her entire family
Were slaughtered
And yet, every morning,
She wakes up and gives
Life to her plants

- Sana Uqba

A damaged building barely stands
And yet inside it, children chant the alphabet
Like a broken, defeated mother
Caring for her kids, **despite her aches and pain**

- Sana Uqba

In a world of 7 billion we are
Left unheard,
Left unsearched
In the dark alleys
of the **third world**

- Sana Uqba

These **delicate tears**
Shake The Throne up above
Do not tell me I am unarmed

- Sana Uqba

God bless the **scars on your hands**
The wrinkles of your skin,
The sweat on your temple and the worry in your eyes,
For they are proof of your
Innate and eternal
Love for me

- Sana Uqba

Faith, my friend,
Is pulling seven family members
From the rubble of your home,
And still thanking God
For every situation

- Sana Uqba

You are the brown of my skin
The pink of my lips
The darkness of my eyes
You are the red in my blood
You are the paint
That created
This art

- Sana Uqba

Why us, mama?
Her henna-tipped fingers
Held my face.
"Others have it worse"
Is there worse than war?
"Yes habibti,
Losing hope," she says

- Sana Uqba

Every time I tried to
Say I love you
An airstrike struck
And drowned out my voice.
Maybe, **next time** she'll hear it

- Sana Uqba

He placed his hand on his heart,
Smiled and bowed;
A humble king
Saluting his queen
In a moment of **peace among the chaos**

- Sana Uqba

Show me your wounds,
"Which one, Doctor?"

- Sana Uqba

Brother, where should we go?
Where do we run?
Where do we hide from the thunder above?
Military raindrops
Destroyed all under the sun
All things known
All things safe,
All familiar faces
Gone.

- Sana Uqba

Rubble rubble
Bombs and trouble,
Buildings burn
And fathers **shovel**

- Sana Uqba

Why don't you come down
And fight us like men?
He pointed and screamed.
"Sit down and roll the dice, son.
Men don't kill"
- Sana Uqba

And all this time
Caged in your love
Trapped in your torment
Tortured in your heat;
Flight is never an option

- Sana Uqba

My heart rests restless
On **tragic sands**
Bruised at the view
Of engulfed homes,
I stand

- Sana Uqba

The news speaks of conflict and war
But I wake up to the **voice of my mother**
And the sweet smell of her hands at work.
How can I not feel anything
But peace?

- Sana Uqba

They ask me how I resist?
I say, I **wave my flag**

- Sana Uqba

It's those damn rebels
Who forced that damn coalition
To back our damn gov -
"Doctor, please stop.
I am **here to be healed**"

- Sana Uqba

How do we win this war, Baba?
"Come here, my sweet"
He walked me out onto the yard
My mother sat on the desert ground
A pot clasped between her feet,
She held a wooden baton
And with it she beat
Till sweat trickled down her sweet cheeks
"Look at this," he said
"Tell me, do these soldiers have
The same **resilience**
As a Yemeni mother
Making *aseed?"

- Sana Uqba

*Wheat based dish

89

He travels across the country
In and out of homes
Weaving like the **cliffs of Hadramawt**
An unwanted guest,
From the darkest nightmares
He is Malik al-Mawt;
The angel of death

- Sana Uqba

Hate is a foreign word
From a **foreign** land
It has no home here

- Sana Uqba

He kissed her temple
And placed his hand
Over her worried ears.
And just like that
The **war was over**

- Sana Uqba

Baba, **where is the Ummah** of Muhammad?
"Arguing on Facebook"
Even Abdullah?
"He found another master"

- Sana Uqba

So, **what of the children**
Who yearn to hear
The voices of their teachers
And those eager
To graduate, like you and I

- Sana Uqba

It rained down on us
And like always we stayed
and splashed around. This time,
to the sounds of F-16s
"Dandeni," she told me
"Lose yourself in the music," she said,
Moments before I lost her in the rubble.

- Sana Uqba

We only seek
Asylum and refuge,
We seek
Safety, security, and education,
We do not seek
Terror targets, sir

- Sana Uqba

This filter
Tells me I'm snapping from
"The **world's worst humanitarian crisis**"

- Sana Uqba

What is war?
"War is that which forces doctors to rely on
Prayers before medication"

- Sana Uqba

Let's take a walk
"But, it's not safe," she said.
He offered **his hand**

- Sana Uqba

Honey, we make music
Out of empty fuel cans
And dance to the sound
Of faraway bullets.
We **celebrate death**
When it challenges us to duel

- Sana Uqba

Our chests warm,
We locked necks
His ear plugged into mine
And I could hear the waves
Of the Arabian Sea.
What a beautiful **seashell**

- Sana Uqba

Architecture of a thousand years
Tainted by corpses thrown along the horizon,
Our **skyline** is to die for

- Sana Uqba

With every hit
I would plead Your name,
So who do I call then
After the **ninety-ninth strike?**

- Sana Uqba

Strap those **roses** up
And launch them
At the enemy.
Darling, we love
We don't fight.

- Sana Uqba

In my mind
I've killed them **a thousand times**
And injected them with the pain
That I see in her eyes

- Sana Uqba

What's your name?
"Mathloom."
Your mother named you oppression?
"No.
The day I pulled her out of the rubble,
I named myself Mathloom."

- Sana Uqba

Conflict is building up
Like **thunder and lightening**
In a land that see's little rain.
This is not what we prayed for.

- Sana Uqba

It's been **three years.**
I need to touch its sand
And breathe its air,
I crave the wetness of the ocean
I once played in

- Sana Uqba

Suction.
It feels like suction,
Like a black hole;
A heavy,
Heavy chest;
Like you're being drip-fed air.
That's what death feels like

- Sana Uqba

She stood
Almost unfazed by the side of
What was once her home.
Zainab began to move forward,
Moments later, she had conquered
The rubble, standing high above,
"What do you see?" the reporter asked.
"The same as she saw," Zainab said.
"I see **nothing but beauty**"

- Sana Uqba

You cannot
Break a people
That believe in the
Justice of the afterlife
- Sana Uqba

Every Friday
Is the **Friday of Karama.**
Men raise janbiyas
Women raise their voices
To ululate
For our fallen grooms.
No one is forgotten here

- Sana Uqba

When the guns stop firing
And the missiles stop falling
When the headlines disappear
And mourners stop mourning
When the curtains start to open
And children begin to fill the streets
Do you know what will happen?
"What?" she asked, with a glimmer of hope.
Our kids will pick up toy guns
And begin shooting each other.
And that is the real **tragedy of war**, *ya binty.

- Sana Uqba

*My daughter

The **angel of death**
Often has tea at our house,
It's almost like
He's becoming one of the family

- Sana Uqba

Get the shovel
"No," I screamed,
"What's the point?
We'll have to **bury** her again anyway"

- Sana Uqba

Killers on the ground
Murderers high above,
Even **star gazing** is a danger
For people like us

- Sana Uqba

He sat on a step,
His skinny legs folded up like a folding chair;
His hand on his walking stick
His crown on his head,
Wisdom of a thousands years
Occupied his teary-eyes
As he put away the newspaper.
"These people praise
My Prophet's name?
One day, I will complain to
Muhammad himself."

- Sana Uqba

His voice
Haunts every room
And every corner
Of my memory.
He is here

- Sana Uqba

Open the window,
Let me hear what **senseless money**
Sounds like

- Sana Uqba

Take me home
Where water is valued
Above crystals
And crystal waters
Tease the words of poets and minstrels
Take me home
Where in poor faces
I find content
And in empty pockets
I find generous hearts
Where one beautiful soul arrives
As soon as a beautiful soul departs
Take me home
To the home of beauty
To the set of a romance movie
Where the sun kisses the ocean
And the ocean kisses the land
Where I witness the meeting
Of long lost brothers
On the horizon
Blue from the sadness
The same sadness I feel
Away from your sands
Take me home
One your wings I will perch
You and I

Will glide and travel
Through the skies
In search of my home
Take me home
Where bees create the sweetest honey
Where streets
Hustle and bustle
Like bees on honey
Where beauty of trees
Depend not on leaves
Where desert sand
Accomodates the green
Take me home
Where life is introduced
To the lifeless
Where the rich travel
To meet the priceless
Take me home
Where the sea protects the mountains
And the mountains protect the people
From evil
Take me home where there is no evil
Take me home
To the land of prophecy
To the land of the future and history
Take me home

Take me home
To the scene etched in my mind
In waking moments
In deepest sleeps
In waking moments
In deepest dreams
I smell its fragrance,
Its air I breathe
A traitor migrant
Its trust I seek
Take me home
Let me embrace your warmth
Let me kiss your sweet forehead
And run through your shores
Take me home
Take me home
Where my tears mix perfectly
With your water
Take me home
To my homeland
To the land
Where my home stands
A four-sided museum of my fairy tale
To the place I first tried
And place I first failed
Take me home

To the land of free minds
And the home of free hearts
Where all I see
Are the eyes of my brother
And all I feel is the touch of a mother
Take me home
Where all my memories gather
As one
Where my heart first spoke to you
O' lover
Take me home
To where life will end and life begun
Take me home
Where the pistol was first shot
Before I embarked
Where the first poem I wrote
Was the beat
Of my heart
Take me home
Please take me home
To where I belong.

- Sana Uqba

Let me ask you a question
What do you know about Yemen?
What do you know
Other than al-Qaeda
And marriage as early as seven?
What do you know about my country
And my people
For starters,
That you're a descendent of
My people?

I'm getting sick and tired
Of this blatant ignorance
And these papers claiming
We breed terrorists;
Train and arm them,
Yeah, I'm armed
Witness as
With this pen in my hand
I go all crazy and militant.

Again with the question,
What do you know about Yemen?
This ain't a poem
This is more of a
History lesson.

We had rulers dating back
As early as Qahtan
Christians pick up the Bible
And Muslims, the Quran
Because it's mentioned in both,
Hard facts, its not a mystery
Say what you want,
Try as you might;
You can't erase history.

We established the earliest trade
Ever known to man
Spices and frankincense
Were sent across the land.
Don't ever look down on us;
Know where you stand
Why we're always made to feel
Inferior, I'll never understand.
Considering all we've given
And the input we've had,
Why we've been left behind
And forgotten,
I'll never understand

What do you know about Yemen?
Believe it or not,

The birthplace of your own
Personal heaven
That mocha you purchase
From your cafe every day
Is named after a Yemeni city
Where coffee was first traded

And don't talk to me about MEDC's
When we built the first skyscrapers
The world's ever seen
Made entirely of mud brick
And still standing today.
Please don't talk to me about
Women's oppression and inequality
When the most respected female
Leader of all-time
Was a born and bred Yemeni.

I am the land of the Arabs
The foundation and root of the Middle East
I am the forgotten jewel of Arabia
I am Yemen.
What do you know about me?

- Sana Uqba

I suffer from your love and
I am in love with this suffering
But as that fighter once said;
I see beauty in everything
*Mawtini, I see beauty in the pain
You and I are witnessing.
Beyond the grey clouds, the dead eyes
The death cries and white shrouds,
I see you standing there
Waiting for me to see past the darkness,
See I know you are full of heart while I
Have been heartless
Towards you, Mawtini
Forgive me
For painting your earth with blood and limbs,
When you showered me with love
I clipped your wings,
Mawtini,
I am ashamed
For allowing politics to come
Between me and my king
And you are my king, Mawtini.
Like a crown I place you above all,
*Ya taaj al raas
Here I stand, answering your call
Let me fix you,

*My nation
*O' crown on my head

127

Heal the wounds of this war,
Mawtini
I swear, I swear
I would kiss
Every spec of sand that covers you
This is a romance between lovers,
Let's not get political
And I know I sound crazy
But have you ever heard of a love story
That's logical?
Mawtini, habibi
I know you can hear me.
I can hear you breathe.. Slowly
Please believe me,
When I say I will never again let you fall
And never again will you have to descend and crawl
To find dignity,
You are dignified,
The peak of nobility,
Your karama is crystallised,
And no filthy hands can
Break you,
No filthy brands can
Shake you,
No backwards man
Can make you regress,

You define worth
And without you I am worthless,
I salute you
As I rise to your service.
My mother prepared me.
My mother prepared me,
To receive every bullet
They've pierced you with for decades,
Every missile, every bomb
That helped decay
Your age,
Every lie, every curse
Scribbled onto the pages
Of your history.
Of our bloody history.
I am here to erase your pain,
I am here to clear your haze,
Make sense of your daze,
Mawtini
I am here to serve you again.
Let me wave your colours, Mawtini,
Let me wave those colours
To the beat heard from the dying breaths
Of our martyrs,
To the tunes heard from the
*Helalhel of our mothers,

*Ulalation

And we will gather
Around the destructive fire they lit
Listening to folktales from our fathers,
Who will speak of a nation.
A great, great nation
That pulled through the storm
And stood strong in congregation
And welcomed martyrdom with ululation
Mawtini,
Celebrate.
Mawtini,
Celebrate
Your existence
Through the wars,
And the blood,
And the bombs,
And the battles,
You
Still
Breathe.
Mawtini.
Stand up, you are still breathing.

- Sana Uqba

War& Love

War& Love

132

ABOUT THE AUTHOR

Sana Uqba is a British-Yemeni journalist, writer and poet who has worked with a range of international and national broadcasters where she has produced television shows and documentaries looking at current affairs. She currently works with a number of online media platforms, writing news, cultural and political articles on the Middle East, with a particular focus on Yemen and the GCC region.

Sana has been writing poetry from a young age and began sharing her work online under the pseudonym **Sanasiino** before being invited to recite spoken word poetry at cultural and political events across the United Kingdom.

War & Love is Sana's first published book.

War
& Love
SANA UQBA

SANA UQBA

ISBN: 1999586603
ISBN-13: 978-1999586607
(Sana Uqba)

22000843R00081

Printed in Great Britain
by Amazon